The Lancashire Witches

by

W. R. Mitchell

Pendle stands,
Rouwnd cop, survaiying all ye wilde moore lands,
And Malkin Toure, a little cottage where
Report makes caitive witches meete to swearr
Their homage to ye divell, and contrive
The deaths of men and beasts . . .

Dalesman Books
1984

THE DALESMAN PUBLISHING COMPANY LTD.
CLAPHAM, via Lancaster, LA2 8EB
Based partly on the author's "Lancashire Witch Country"
First published in this format 1984

© W. R. Mitchell, 1984

ISBN: 0 85206 776 3

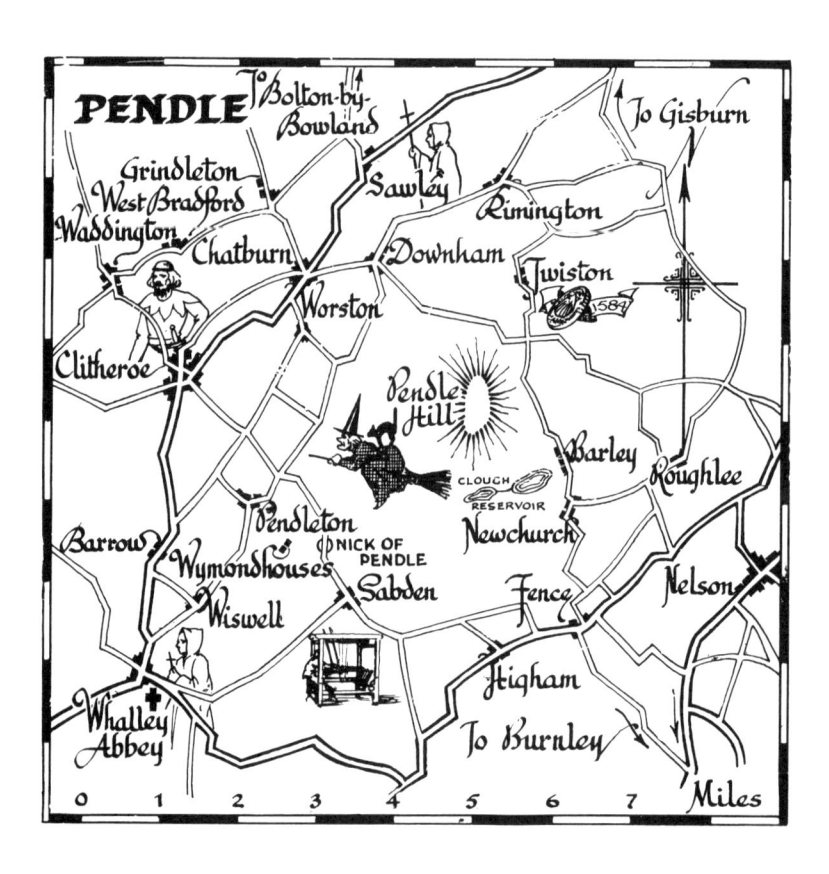

Printed by Fretwell & Brian Ltd.,
Healey Works, Goulbourne Street, Keighley, West Yorkshire BD21 1PZ

Contents
and
Illustrations

OUTSIDE THE CHAPEL AT MARTIN TOP

Wisewomen or Witches? 5
On and Around Pendle 6
Characters in the Witch Story 12
Witchcraft Around Pendle 15
On Trial at Lancaster 24
Where Was Malkin Tower? 25
The Boy who Found Witches 26
Witch Country Literature 29
Last thoughts about Witches 31
Nineteen Names 32

★ ★ ★

Front cover photograph of Pendle Hill from Longridge Fell by Norman Duerden.
All uncredited photographs by the author. Map by E. Jeffrey.

PHOTO: C. HARRINGTON

**Pendle Hill, viewed from
the neighbourhood of Sawley.**

Wisewomen or Witches?

IN THE YEAR 1613, the clerk to the judges of Lancaster Assizes — one Thomas Potts — published a record he had made of the trial of witches from Pendle Forest. It was a time when witchcraft interested almost everyone, and many trials took place throughout the land. It so happens that the Pendle Witches had a special chronicler in Mr. Potts, and that early last century his account was re-published, with the enthusiastic support of none other than Sir Walter Scott.

Another version appeared in 1845 under the auspices of the Chetham Society of Manchester, and then came the work that added the dash of romance necessary if a theme is to capture public imagination. A novelist called Harrison Ainsworth penned *The Lancashire Witches* (1848). It was dedicated to James Crossley, president of the Chetham Society, with a note that this "romance" had been written at his suggestion. Scarcely a book written about the Pendle Country — or indeed about Lancashire — since that time has failed to mention the Pendle Witches. They have surely become the most famous witches in the land.

In our own century, interest in them was re-kindled by a splendid novel by Robert Neill entitled *Mist over Pendle*. Neill paid his own special tribute to Thomas Potts, "Sometime Clerk to the Judges in The Circuit of the North Parts Who in November, 1612, at his Lodging in Chancery Lane, wrote of the Late WONDERFUL DISCOVERIE OF WITCHES in the Countie of Lancaster."

This present booklet is for those who, while visiting Pendle, have more than a passing interest in the folk who were said to have practised the devilish art of witchcraft — visitors who, being very romantic, might mistake the crow being blown along by a wind, under the scudding clouds, for a distant witch on her broomstick! There are much more comprehensive works, notably Walter Bennett's *The Pendle Witches* (1947) and Peel and Southern's *The Trials of the Lancashire Witches* (1969).

Were they really witches? Or just wisewomen, who normally cured people and animals using countless remedies in an age before well-developed medical and veterinary services, and who in this case used their formidable appearances and reputations to do a little begging as well? We will never know . . .

On and Around Pendle

HARRISON AINSWORTH'S romance, *The Lancashire Witches*, contains some colourful word pictures of the Pendle countryside. It begins with eight watchers by the beacon on Pendle, with a further two stationed on either side of the north-eastern extremity of the mountain. What did these two see? "One looked over the castled heights of Clithero; the woody eminences of Bowland; the bleak ridges of Thornley; the broad moors of Bleasdale; the Trough of Bolland, and Wolf Crag; and even brought within his ken the black fells overhanging Lancaster. The other tracked the stream called Pendle Water, almost from its source amid the neighbouring hills, and followed its windings through the leafless forest, until it united its waters to those of the Calder, and swept on in swifter and clearer current, to wash the base of Whalley Abbey . . ."

We who are elated at the prospect of trudging across Pendle cannot truly imagine the feelings of people of Ainsworth's time. He was born in Manchester in 1805, and died at Reigate in 1882. In his novel he imagined events in the 17th century. After detailing the main features of the landscape to be viewed from Pendle, he wrote: "Dreary was the prospect on all sides, black moor, bleak fell, straggling forest, intersected with sullen streams as black as ink, with here and there a small tarn, or moss-pool, with waters of the same hue. These constituted the chief features of the scene. The whole district was barren and thinly populated."

It is fascinating to read Harrison Ainsworth's description of an area which is now characterised by a conurbation of mill towns, and from which on a winter night Pendle is bathed by orange light. He writes of Read Hall, "situated on an eminence forming part of the heights of Padiham," and facing a wide valley, "watered by the Calder, and consisting chiefly of barren tracts of moor and forest land, bounded by the high hills near Accrington and Rossendale. On the left, some half-dozen miles off, lay Burnley, and the greater part of the land in this direction, being unenclosed and thinly peopled, had a dark, dreary look, that served to enhance the green beauty of the well-cultivated district on the right."

The eye returns again and again to Pendle. This famous Hill — at 1,832 feet it falls short of true mountain status — sprawls over 25 square miles and thus stands up to the fierce westerly gales without rocking. It appears, when viewed from the Ribble Valley, to culminate in an edge as fine as a knife blade; the reality is that atop the mountain is a plateau of considerable size, with peat and bogs, especially bogs. Pendle is a wet hill, the home of wind, rain and cloud. Stukeley wrote in the 18th century of the "vast black mountain . . . the morning weather glass of the country people." Camden mentioned its crest as being "black and cloudly."

Clitheroe, showing the castle keep.

Earlier visitors to Downham stared at the Hill from the lowlands and listened to local tales about the grandeur of Pendle. Most of those who wrote about the district repeated the rhyming couplet which claims that "Ingleborough, Pendle Hill and Penigent (Penyghent) bee the highest hills between Scotland and Trent." It has many variants. Michael Drayton reported that it was among "the highest hills that be," and Thomas Hurtley, a Craven historian and topographer, put the height at 3,411 feet. Much later, when Pendle's true height had been determined — and the Lakeland mountains had been rightly acknowledged as the highest in England — men wrote of the character of Pendle. Dr. Spencer T. Hall said the Hill was "more like a living creature stretch'd in sleep, its couch the forest, and its cope the sky."

It is amusing to study the shape of Pendle and compare it with more mundane objects. It has been seen to resemble a large brown ridge tent, with one pole shorter than the other. It has also been compared with an upturned boat. Pendle, a tabular hill, has kept its shape and size because the summit layer of rock is hard, weather-resisting gritstone. Pendle stands, "rouwnd cop, survaiying all ye wilde moore lands," as James, the parson-poet, noted in the 17th century.

Two contrasting impressions of Pendle were presented in Harrison Ainsworth's *The Lancashire Witches*. Nicholas Assheton, and Potts, a Londoner, stood on Whalley Nab, and Nicholas cried enthusiastically: "I love Pendle Hill." He enjoyed the sight from any angle, "whether from this place, where I see it from end to end, from its lowest point to its highest; from Padiham, where it frowns upon me; from Clitheroe, where it smiles; or from Downham where it rises in full majesty before me — from all points and under all aspects, whether robed in mist or radiant with sunshine, I delight in it." Potts thought that Hampstead Heath was wild enough for any civilised purpose. He considered that Pendle had no other recommendation than its size. It was "a great, brown, ugly, lumpy mass, without beauty or form or any striking character." Potts said to Nicholas Assheton: "Every man to his taste, squire."

Though Pendle is not quite a mountain, it cannot be ignored. It is individual, distinctive. North of the Hill, the Ribble Valley broadens, like gentle parkland, though the Clitheroe by-pass detracts mightily from the natural beauty. Calder, to the south, has its source in the wild little gorge at Cliviger, a few miles from Burnley. It is ignored by Pendle Water, draining the summit area of the Hill, and now flows close to Higham, then Padiham, cleansing itself a little before entering the Ribble near Whalley. A third river to make its mark on the Witch Country is the sparkling Hodder, the main watercourse of Bowland.

South-east of Pendle, low in the valley, is the conurbation of mill towns — Colne, Barrowford, Nelson, Brierfield, Burnley, Padiham. They do not dominate the Pendle landscape, and a slight industrial haze removes the hard lines from the townscape. Pendle's popularity as a summit to be visited is, in part, the creation of generations of mill folk who found on the high ground a place for recreation and rural pleasures. Where streams and rivers gurgled from the Hill, small mills were established, away from the main conurbation, and so there are chimneys within a mile or so of Pendle summit. Sabden has some elements of a mill town and sprawls on the slope leading to Pendle's Nick.

Pendle is divided into moors. The traditional sheep were Lonks, a breed developed on the lower Pennines and favoured by the hill farmers of West Yorkshire and East Lancashire alike. Halifax was a traditional marketing centre. Now the Lonk blood has been blended with that of the Swaledale. Walls are absent from the higher parts of Pendle, and so the heaf-going instinct of the sheep is cherished. They can be relied upon to stay in certain limited areas. A shepherd who looked after the sheep on the Barley side of Pendle had a special duty at haytime. He would sit on top of the Hill, within sight of the haymakers, and wave a black flag if a storm was blowing up from the direction of the coast. In this way the farmers had two hours' notice of bad weather. The Hill completely blocked a view of the sky in that direction.

Pendle from Whitehough *(Photo: Kenneth Oldham).*

Pendle is plainlooking; there is scarcely a tree upon it. In Norman times, it was a forest, but Pendle Forest was far removed from today's idea of a forest — of regimented rows of conifers, fairly newly-planted, carefully tended by a small army of workpeople, and systematically felled. In the old days, it was an area set aside as a chase for wild animals, with a fairly low coverlet of native timber: birch and alder, with oak on the lower ground. There were also forests at Rossendale, Trawden and Bowland.

The climate often gives Pendle a capping of cloud or mist. The Hill is seen best when the slopes are an ever-varying pattern of sunshine and shadow. It has been said: "If you can see Pendle, it's going to rain; if you can't see Pendle, it's raining!" On at least three occasions in recorded times there have been vast eruptions — known as water brasts — from the flanks of the Hill. Writers have commented upon them since Camden, the historian, noted that "Pendle is chiefly famous for the great damage done to the lower grounds about it heretofore by the fall of water that issued from it." One of these terrifying eruptions created Brast Clough. Water brasts were noted in 1580, 1669 and 1870, and of the second it was related that there was a "mighty torrent gushing out in such quantities and so suddenly that it made a brast a yard high and continued running for about two hours."

If you call this great hump "Pendle Hill" you are using the word "hill" three times in different ways. Pen itself was the Ancient British word for hill. The Saxons added their own term, which ultimately gave the name Pendle. It was until recently called Penhill. To this wild country, haunt of the Brigantes — a brave and warlike Iron Age people — came the Romans. They constructed an important military centre at Ribchester, though not much of it can be seen today for since Roman times the Ribble has shifted its bed, and the parish church occupies part of the old camp. Pendle folk could look down on evidence of Roman settlement and enterprise, for a road from Ribchester ran through the Aire Gap to Ilkley. Paulinus, stern, dark chaplain to the Christian queen of a heathen Northumbria, is reputed to have preached in this district, which is very likely, for the bounds of Anglian Northumbria were gradually extended to the western sea.

When the Normans arrived, Clitheroe became the important local centre. A castle appeared on the limestone knoll, and the de Lacy family established a forest on Pendle between 1070 and 1114. It covered 25,000 acres, and stretched from Pendle Hill to Colne. Cattle farms or "vaccaries" were being established in the 13th century. The wild boar were among the local fauna up to the early 17th century. Workers lived in clearings in the forest, and the main clearings — five in number — were later known as "booths". They were the nuclei of the villages round Pendle today. The last courts of the Forest Leet were held at the *Four Alls Inn,* Higham.

From the Pendle area were drawn men who fought at Flodden, a decisive battle in the long-played war between England and Scotland. Henry Clifford, of Skipton Castle, mustered the Craven contingent, and

> *From Penigant to Pendle Hill*
> *From Linton to Long Addingham*
> *And all that Craven crofts did 'til*
> *They with the lusty Clifford came.*

The most prominent hills of the North Country formed part of an early warning system in times of national crisis. A bonfire blazing on Pendle would muster the militia and send civilians scuttering for shelter. Then came the age when bonfire denoted important celebrations. One of the largest beacons on Pendle was lighted in June, 1887, when the jubilee of Queen Victoria was celebrated. It was organised by people living in Burnley; they had banded together, formed a committee, and arranged for combustibles to be taken to the summit by twenty horses. Over a thousand people gathered on Pendle on Jubilee Day. The material set alight included 17 tons of coal, a ton of naptha and three barrels of petroleum.

From the crude nature worship of the Celtic folk, to the present day, Pendle has seen many forms of religious worship and superstitious practice. Sun worship is perpetuated by those who climb the Hill to watch for dawn on Midsummer Day. Was the notion that York Minster could be seen in clear weather the Church's answer to the old beliefs? Near Pendle were two famous Cistercian abbeys — Whalley and Sawley. Sadly too close to each other for comfort, each was bedevilled, in the earliest years, by spells of wet weather, which helped the corn to grow quickly but rotted the ears before the harvest.

The Vicar of Whalley once had the spiritual oversight of Pendle Forest. Then, in 1544 "The Chapell of the Blessed Virgin of Pendhill" (sometimes referred to as Pendle Chapel) was consecrated in Goldshaw Booth, though there would have been a chapel in the Forest before this. The "new church" of 1544 (re-built in the 18th century) names an important village, Newchurch-in-Pendle. On the tower is a feature said to represent the all seeing eye of God.

George Fox, founder of the Quaker movement, possibly wearied by the clamour in the valleys, climbed Pendle in 1652. Here he had his famous vision. "I was moved of the Lord to go up to the top of it, which I did with much ado, as it was so very steep and high. When I was come to the top of this hill I saw the sea bordering upon Lancashire; and from the top of this hill the Lord let me see in what places He had a great people to be gathered. As I went down I found a spring of water in the side of the hill, with which I refreshed myself, having eaten or drunk but little in several days before."

Pendle is the right sort of peak for a vision. It is little more than a great elevated platform, the summit remarkable in itself but ideal as a vantage point. Fox, 300 years ago, would have a vista which has since changed in many ways, but which has retained its elemental features. He would be able to see the sun glinting on the Irish Sea, and (if the weather was very clear) the fells of Cumbria, a region where, in coming years, some of his staunchest disciples would be found. He would look to the Bowland fells, and up the Ribble Valley to the outliers of the limestone country — the Three Peaks of Yorkshire — with Ingleborough stealing the attention.

Fox would also see Lancaster, with its grim old castle, where not so many years before the Pendle witches had languished. The founder of Quakerism spent the winter of 1664–5 in the Lancaster dungeons; he had refused to take the oath in open court.

There are times when Pendle's face is in shadow, and the Hill looks a little sad, as though recalling incidents from an age of intolerance. When the great hump of Pendle is sunlit, you think instead of the saints, among them Thomas Jollie, a notable Nonconformist who made Wymondhouses in Pendle a centre of religion for many miles around in the first half of the 17th century. So even as Pendle witches were being slain, men were striving to bring a greater liberality into the way that people thought.

Pendle is included in an area of "outstanding natural beauty" which is centred on Bowland. This designation was made under the National Parks Act, 1949.

Characters in the Witch Story
(presented in alphabetical order)

BANNISTER, Nicholas. A Justice of the Peace, resident at Altham. With another Justice, Roger Nowell, inquired into a meeting of relatives and friends of those who had been taken for trial to Lancaster; the meeting had taken place at Malkin Tower, the home of Old Demdike.

CHATTOX. The nickname of Anne Whittle, who lived in the Greenhead area.

DEMDIKE, Old. The nickname for Elizabeth Southerns, of Malkin Tower. Her home was shared with Elizabeth, her daughter, John Davies, her son-in-law; and their family.

DAVIES (or Device), Alizon. The granddaughter of Old Demdike who was usually engaged in begging (which was not necessarily illegal) and who when required led her virtually blind grandmother about the district. It was Alizon who triggered off the incidents involving the Pendle witches when, while passing through the town of Colne on her way to Trawden Forest, met a pedlar call John Law and, when he became lame, confessed that she had bewitched him.

DAVIES, Elizabeth. The widow of John Davies, who was a victim of Old Chattox.

DAVIES, James. The grandson of Old Demdike.

DAVIES, John. Son-in-law of Old Demdike; he died, claiming that Chattox had bewitched him.

HEWITT, Katherine. She resided at Colne, where she was known as Mouldheels. She was among those who attended the assembly at Malkin Tower on Good Friday.

LAW, Abraham. The son of John Law, the pedlar who was supposedly bewitched by Alizon. Though she confessed, and was forgiven by John, Abraham insisted on taking Alizon and close relatives to the magistrate, Roger Nowell, thus putting in train the legal process that led to trial at Lancaster.

NOWELL, Roger. He lived at Read Hall, and was a Justice of the Peace. According to Thomas Potts, who had a high regard for his superiors, Nowell was "a very religious honest Gentleman, painefull in the seruice of his Countrey." Nowell was interred at Whalley.

NUTTER, Alice. The name of this gentlewoman, who lived at Roughlee, appeared on the list of those who assembled at Malkin Tower on Good Friday. There has been much speculation about why such a wealthy and influential person should be found associating with the rougher elements of Pendle society.

POTTS, Thomas. Master Potts, Clerk to the Judges in "The Circuit of the North Parts", kept a record of the Trials of the Witches and immortalised this particular Pendle group by compiling a book (1613) entitled "The Wonderfvll Discoverie of Witches in the Covntie of Lancaster." Indeed, he mentioned 19 witches, for the Pendle group was not alone in being tried for witchcraft in 1612.

PRESTON, Jennet. She lived at Gisburn, was charged (at York) with murder by witchcraft, and was acquitted. Then tried for murder of Thomas Lister and found guilty. Hanged at York.

REDFEARN, Anne. Daughter of Old Chattox. Married to Thomas; they lived with Chattox.

SOUTHERNS, Elizabeth. Old Demdike, of Malkin Tower. Questioned by Roger Nowell and detained as a witch.

WHITTLE, Anne. Nicknamed Old Chattox.

A "Witch Window" at Worston.

Witchcraft Around Pendle

SIR WILLIAM PELHAM wrote to Lord Conway in 1634: "The greatest news from the country is of a huge pack of witches, which are lately discovered in Lancashire, whereof, 'tis said, nineteen are condemned, and that there are at least sixty already discovered, and yet daily there are more revealed." In our book, special attention is given to the witches around Pendle Hill. Early in the 17th century, witches were on everybody's minds. A Scottish group had been introduced in *Macbeth* by one Will Shakespeare in 1606, less than a decade after no less a personage than King James had written about (and, of course, against) witchcraft in what became a standard work, *Daemonologie*. Less than a decade after Shakespeare's play, "witches" were found to be everywhere!

If Elizabeth (Bessie) Whittle, the daughter of Old Chattox, had not broken into the "fire-house" of Malkin Tower near Newchurch early in March, 1612, the famous Pendle witch trials are unlikely to have been held. For years rumours had been circulating around Pendle about women who were in league with the Devil. A plain man's insurance against evil influences was a charm, or several charms, for the spirits of darkness were many and varied. Rowan wood was recommended as a protection for stock or property against these harmful crones. Witch charms included stones, holed at the centre, strung so that they could be hung up or draped from the neck.

The farmers and traders of the Pendle country had occasional brief encounters with Demdike, Chattox and their offspring, who had reputedly given their souls to the Devil. Superficially, they were beggars, and it was best to give them a trifle and let them shuffle on their way to the next hapless people, or a cow might develop sudden violent pains, the limbs of loved ones begin to waste away, or some other calamity occur. There was eventually "a general murmuring of the populace" about the families.

Not all beggars were counted as witches, and this was just as well. In the early years of the 17th century this remote, thinly populated, Pendle countryside had many beggars, rogues and vagabonds who were continually leaving their parishes to plague others. A good whipping, or worse, was administered, and the miscreants were usually returned post haste to their home acres, there to be found some gainful occupation if work was available and the people had a mind to do it. Many, alas, were unemployable.

Above: Pendle from Downham *(Photo: Clifford Robinson)*
Below: Roughlee Old Hall.

Below: A grave of a member of the Nutter family at Newchurch.

Elizabeth Whittle, who slipped into the Malkin "fire-house", was the daughter of a widow named Anne Whittle. Many Pendlesiders would not have recognised that name. Anne was nicknamed Chattox after her maiden name of Chadwick. She lived in a hovel on Greenhead land, near Fence. In 1612 she was not a very pleasant person to behold. Chattox was about 80 years old; the passing of time had dealt ungracefully with her. She was "a very old withered spent and decreped creature, her sight almost gone . . . Her lips ever chattering and talking; but no man knew what." It was best not to linger when Old Chattox was about, and only one woman was feared more: equally decrepit Mother Demdike, of Malkin Tower. These two had spawned most of the "witches" of the area.

What came over Elizabeth when she left the Whittles' cottage? To pilfer Demdike property was dangerous and, to a person as adroit as Elizabeth, quite unnecessary. Many other courses were possible. She left with "all or most of their linen clothes, half a peck of cut oatmeal, and a quantity of meal, all worth twenty shillings and more." Demdike was surnamed Southerns, but her daughter Elizabeth had married John Davies, or Device (as written at the trial). He died claiming that Chattox had bewitched him. Living at Malkin Tower were the unruly outcome of the marriage — Alizon, James and Jenet, in that order of age.

Chattox's eyesight had almost gone. Demdike was blinder than a bat: shifty and shuffling, wandering about the countryside with the help of her grandchildren. Demdike was "a general agent for the deiull in all these partes," and at 80 years old she would doubtless have been proud of the status. Daughter Elizabeth was as wild "as they mak 'em," even in a remote district like Pendle. There were times when she could act reasonably, though her face was disturbing, with one eye set up and the other eye inclined downwards. To observe that she was mentally upset is to use the kindest term. Elizabeth Davies had fits which roused her to a passion which neither she nor anyone else could master. The passion was sometimes spent on illicit relationships. In this, Elizabeth Davies was following a pattern set by Old Demdike herself. Demdike had been promiscuous in her younger day, and Christopher Holgate, her son, was illegitimate. Christopher was spoken of as a witch, but in 1612 he was married. He and his wife lived fairly quietly, away from the ancestral hovel.

Alizon, the grand-daughter, was sane enough but she had a roughish bringing-up, and her standards were apparently not very high. If Alizon worked it was to beg from all and sundry. Sometimes she was joined by her brother James, a lad who had a childish mind throughout his life. Alizon and her sister Jenet, who was only nine years old in 1612, were a sad product of environment and family influence. Both were to be branded as witches.

Elizabeth got clear of Malkin Tower with her spoils. She was unwise enough to wear some of the clothes next Sunday. Alizon Davies recognised "a band and coif." The information was reported to the Greave of Pendle

Forest, and he passed it on to the local magistrate, Roger Nowell, who — like all the Justices of the time — had his hands full with matters related to the Poor Law. There were other inexplicable incidents, and people began to recall the alleged bewitching of the Nutters, father and son, who lived at Greenhead.

Roger Nowell (1551–1623) enjoyed his work of law enforcement; he was a meticulous person who revelled in complex legal matters. Most days of the week you would find him at Read Hall, between Padiham and Whalley. On Sundays he occupied the big, imposing pew — a home from home — he had made in the church at Whalley. It was to become known as The Cage because of its many bars. Roger Nowell had heard tales of Pendle "wise women," but there had been little on which he could act. Now (as Potts, reporter of the trial, was to write) this "very religious honest Gentleman . . . tooke upon him to enter into the particular examination of these suspected persons: And . . . made such a discovery of them as the like hath not been heard of."

Roger Nowell had Elizabeth brought before him, and he inquired into her misdeed. As a result, she was committed to gaol at Lancaster, which meant an almost airless dungeon in the grim old castle above the Lune. A landowner in West Close, where she had been living, had to pay part of the cost of having extra clothes sent to her. She had already opened up the subject of supposed Pendle witchcraft. At the inquiry held at Read Hall, the family from Malkin Tower was represented by young Alizon. She could not put up much of a defence when Elizabeth, realising her personal cause was lost, began to smear the Davies' with accusations of witchcraft.

Old Demdike was incriminated, and as Roger Nowell gave Alizon a thorough, at times threatening, interrogation, Alizon blurted out some wild admissions, among them that grandmother had tried to persuade her to become a witch. Old Demdike had bewitched a cow which John Nutter, of Bullhole Farm, had asked her to cure (an unlikely story, for no-one was likely to have truck with a supposed witch if the health of an animal was involved), and there was a day when Demdike charmed a can of milk. A slab of butter appeared in it! Alizon, who cannot have had much idea of the activities of her grandmother, even mentioned a day, two years before, when Richard Baldwin, of Wheetland, had been cursed. A year later he lost a child, and Alizon was sure this had been due to witchcraft.

Roger Nowell was delighted with this information, which he should not have heeded without substantiation. He apparently made no efforts to confirm or deny the tales. He had already gathered information about Alizon, who had been heading for Trawden Forest on a begging mission, and was close to Colne, when she met a Halifax pedlar name John Law and asked him if he would sell her some pins. Law had refused, and said he did not want his pack stolen. Annoyed at the accusation, Alizon cursed him, and both walked on. The pedlar did not go far, collapsing from a seizure which paralysed him down one side and temporarily robbed him of his speech. Moved to a handy ale-house, this pedlar — so recently "a verie able sufficient stout man of Bodie and a goodly man of stature" — complained bitterly that "he was pricked with knives, elsons and sickles."

It seems that Alizon, overcome with remorse, had called to see him, but the sight of the suffering man amazed her. She looked, speechless, and then walked away. Abraham Law, the pedlar's son, attended his father and muttered to the authorities about witchcraft, naming Alizon Davies. She was brought to see the pedlar and — still no doubt flustered — the lass confessed that she had bewitched him. When she asked him to forgive her, he agreed. There was nothing subtle about the speech or manner of Alizon Davies, for she had grown up in a rough, unlettered household, being only a few shades removed from an animal.

She had been taken to Read Hall — to the panelled dignity and comfort of Roger Nowell's house — in the company of her deformed, depraved mother and her simpleton brother, James. Nowell gathered evidence, a good deal of it suspect, about family witchcraft. The Devil had bought her soul, said Alizon, for she had met a black dog when she was walking to "the Rough Lee"; this was her familiar spirit, and it had been responsible for the sudden affliction of the pedlar. Brother James had been easily persuaded to open up on the subject, and grandly mentioned that Alizon had confessed to bewitching a child of Henry Bulcock. Old Demdike was "blackened" by her daughter, who said she had a witch mark (made when the devil drew blood) upon her.

Alizon thought of the clan at West Close, and particularly of Chattox, and told of weird doings which had involved them: of Chattox murdering four men, causing the death of a cow, spoiling some ale, and charming milk. The crowning point came when she accused Chattox of bewitching Alizon's father when he stopped paying Chattox some meal (was the meal to ensure protection for his family?). Chattox had also bewitched Anne, the daughter of Anthony Nutter of Newchurch, and a child of John Moor of Higham had died six months after a Chattox spell had been cast.

That March, Roger Nowell had a mass of evidence of events which he could easily put down to witchcraft, and he did not bother to spoil a good story by making further inquiries. Early in April, he was ready to confront the two most famous witches — Demdike and Chattox — and again he showed his mastery at breaking down witnesses, so that they blurted out the evidence he most wanted to hear. Chattox was in the company of a daughter, Anne Redfern, who — alone — remained composed and did not hurl wild accusations about.

The redoubtable Demdike admitted to being an agent of the Devil. It happened (she said) 20 years before, when she was a on begging expedition. As she returned home, and was at a stone-pit near Newchurch, a spirit in the form of a boy wearing a black and brown coat accosted her, and she gave him

Left: The tower at Newchurch, with an oval feature (well below the clock) said to represent the all-seeing eye of God. Right: Greenhead.

her soul. The spirit was Tibb, and she did not call upon him for five or six years. Then, appearing as a brown dog, Tibb sucked her blood. She had been asleep at the time, wearing only a smock, and with a child on her knee. As she awoke, she had only enough time to cry: "Jesus save my child." Fear kept her from saying: "Jesus save me." For the eight following weeks, she had been "stark mad."

Chattox said her life as a witch had begun when "a Thing like a Christian man" visited her. There were other visits in succeeding years. She agreed to part with her soul, and acquired a familiar spirit, "Fancy". Deeds she had committed with the help of Fancy were specified. Fancy, who had appeared to her occasionally like a gaping bear, had taken "most of her sight."

"Demdike told Roger Nowell the "speediest way to take a man's life away by Witchcraft." It involved an effigy — a picture "of Clay, like unto the shape of the person whom they mean to kill." This should be dried out. What treatment it received would depend on how a witch intended to afflict a victim. Illness in a specific place could be assured if the appropriate place was pricked with "a Thorne or Pinne". The wasting away of a part of a victim could be assured by burning that part of the effigy. "And when they would have the whole body to consume away, then take the remnant of the sayd Picture, and burne it: and so thereupon, by that meanes, the body shall die."

Roger Nowell had his facts and his fancies; his depositions and his confessions, with each family ranged against the other, unburdening themselves of the pent-up feelings of the years. There was enough evidence to commit Demdike, Chattox, Alizon and Anne Redfern to Lancaster. They went through the heathered Trough of Bowland to the fortress and gaol at the county town by the Lune, and here they had to languish until the next Assizes in August. Before the Assize opened, Demdike had died.

The Pendle countryside had not been purged of witches to the magistrate's satisfaction. He heard of a Good Friday gathering of people at Malkin Tower. Roger Nowell might have levelled a theft charge, for James had stolen a "roasted wether" (young male sheep) for the feast. Nowell smelt witchcraft. Three members of the Davies family, Elizabeth, James and Jenet, remained in the area, and another pack of witches could be sent along the Trough road to Lancaster. Many of those who attended were rounded up, and James Davies — a half-wit — later began to rant about the spirit or familiar attending his sister, Alizon; of a plan to liberate the four women already committed to gaol (the gaoler was to be killed and the castle blown up!); and of a sinister plot to kill a Mr. Lister of Westby. It had been arranged to hold another get-together the following Good Friday. Meanwhile, this company had dispersed, all leaving the house "in their shapes and likenesses. And they all, by that they were forth of the doors, were gotten on horseback, like unto foals, some of one colour, some of another".

Elizabeth Davies testified to the "witchly" nature of the meeting, and substantiated names given by James. Young Jenet Davies, then nine years old, basically agreed with what had been said, and gave the number of the people present as about 20, two of them men. Elizabeth revealed that her spirit was a grown dog, named "Ball". Of the new crop of witches that Nowell's men harvested on the lower slopes of Pendle Hill, there was a surprise. Alice Nutter of Roughlee, had been at the Good Friday meeting, and she was a gentlewoman, well-educated and wealthy, quite unlike the others of the Malkin coterie. There was no denying that she had been at Malkin Tower (and she herself remained quiet and calm throughout the hearings which followed, hearing herself incriminated as a witch, and doing nothing to deny the charge).

Roger Nowell was glad to have her before him, for there was a boundary grudge between the two families. It is said that Alice's family was glad to see her labelled a witch, because they wished to inherit certain property. Alice joined the other witches at Lancaster Castle, and the utter misery and privation of life in a crowded gaol must have nauseated her. Was her silence for reasons other than witchcraft? Alice was a devout Catholic, at a time when Catholicism was frowned upon in the land. Close relatives of Alice who became Catholic priests had been put to death in those days of religious intolerance. Did Alice call at Malkin Tower, impelled by no other motive than that of being a good neighbour to a family in a time of distress, while she was on her way to an unofficial Catholic meeting? By her silence did she protect other Catholics?

The "witches" who accompanied her to Lancaster were Elizabeth Davies, James Davies, Katherine Hewitt (the wife of a clothier of Colne), Alice Grey, and John and Jane Bulcock. Young Jenet Preston, interrogated at the same time, was sent for trial, but she lived at Gisburn, in Yorkshire, and so she was taken eastwards to York. Judge Altham pronounced judgement upon her on July 27th. She had been charged with killing, by witchcraft, a Mr. Thomas Lister, and of causing great loss to Mr. Leonard Lister. The verdict was "guilty" and Jenet — a hapless individual, who had been found not guilty of the murder of a child the previous year — was executed. Margaret Pearson, of Padiham, was accused of witchcraft, being alleged to have cast a spell on a mare. A Jenet Booth testified that when she had boiled some water at the Pearson's home a toad, or something very much like a toad, had been found in the fire under the pan. Margaret Pearson joined the others at Lancaster.

Roughlee Old Hall.

On Trial at Lancaster

JUDGE ALTHAM, fresh from the Assizes at York, was welcomed to Lancaster on August 16th, and with him was Judge Bromley. They had travelled via Kendal, and reached Lancaster about noon, receiving the calendar from the governor and noting that it contained the names of 19 witches — a remarkable haul. The preliminaries of the trial took place on the Monday. On Tuesday, the sheriff presented the prisoners, and a jury was mustered. In court, as the prosecutor, was Roger Nowell, wallowing in his depositions. The man who was to chronicle these trials for public consumption, Thomas Potts, had arrived from London. As the Clerk of the Court, he kept the official records, and these formed the basis of his book.

Just as a few ignorant, misguided people had been labelled witches, so the Lancaster gathering went under the title of a trial. It was terribly one-sided. The defendants had no professional representation. The Judges might help them from time to time, but on this occasion they did not appear to strain themselves to show the folk from Pendle in a favourable light. The mood of the time was curiously different from that of today, when most of the evidence offered would have been unacceptable.

The first verdicts were Chattox, Elizabeth Davies and James Davies. All were found guilty. All were sentenced to death. Anne Redfern, who had been charged with the murder of Robert Nutter of Greenhead, was found not guilty, but was then charged with the murder of Christopher Nutter. Her plea of "not guilty" was now unacceptable, and she was sentenced to die. Alice Nutter received the death sentence, and one suspects that she accepted it with the stoicism of her earlier appearances before the Law. Katherine Hewitt, indicted in connection with the murder of Ann Foulds, was also judged guilty and a death sentence was proclaimed. John and Jane Bulcock, found not guilty by the jury, were apparently sentenced to death by the Judge!

Alizon Davies — the girl who cursed John Law, the pedlar — was found guilty on her own confession, and death was the natural legal outcome of her crime. Margaret Pearson was allowed to live, but she suffered the humiliation of standing in the pillory at Clitheroe, Whalley, Padiham and Lancaster, on the four market days. A paper showing her offence was to be posted up, and when the public spectacle was over she was to languish in prison at Lancaster for a year. Demdike had escaped. She had died in her cell before the Assizes opened.

Those convicted were hanged on the following day at "the common place of execution nigh unto Lancaster." It was not the end of witchcraft around Pendle, for in 1633 the district between Higham and the Calder was still regarded as active witch country. Three women were summoned before the Law, but were acquitted of a witchcraft charge. There were more witchly doings in the 1680s.

Where Was Malkin Tower?

THE WITCH COUNTRY has its mysteries, and the most tantalising of them is the precise location of Malkin Tower, where Old Demdike lived. It was from Malkin Tower that she, her children and grandchildren set out on their begging expeditions, and to Malkin Tower that Bessie Whittle slunk on that fateful day in March 1612, when her thieving brought into the open the sad story of Pendle witchcraft. Malkin was the setting for the Good Friday gathering of Demdike's relatives and well-wishers, most of whom were rounded up by Roger Nowell. A visit to Malkin was the last social call undertaken by Alice Nutter, of Roughlee, the gentlewoman who found herself accused with the others of witchcraft, and who did not utter a word in her defence.

No-one knows precisely where Malkin Tower stood, though digging has been undertaken here and there in the hope of finding its foundations. The home of Demdike early in the 17th century was not likely to be substantial. It may even have been a building put up for stock or fodder that was converted into living accommodation — and poor accommodation at that — for a growing family who were prepared to rough it. Mr. Walter Bennett, whose brief study of the Pendle witches is a model of painstaking research and scholarship, gives the situation of Malkin Tower as Malkin Field, part of Sadler's Farm, Newchurch-in-Pendle. When I visited Newchurch, a farmer told me of excavations which had taken place nearby. A number of people in the Roughlee and Blacko areas were equally sure that Malkin Tower lay somewhere between these two villages, or maybe a little to the north.

One day the mystery must be solved. Meanwhile, for those who travel eastwards from Pendle there is an added flavour to the journey in the fact that Demdike and her clan knew this area well, and that begging in Trawden

Forest, which lies south-east of Colne, was on their agenda. Blacko would be just another partly-industrialised village at the edge of Lancashire were it not for the upstanding stonework on the rounded hill behind it, which can be seen from a distance and which gives the place some topographical distinction. This is Blacko Tower, also known as "Jonathan's Folly", from Jonathan Stansfield, a Barrowford businessman, who had it erected in the 1890s. Some visitors like to think of it as a haunt of witches — especially as a nearby farm is called Malkin Tower on the detailed maps of the area. It is significant only as a viewpoint and because it marks the boundaries of Pendle Forest.

The Boy who Found Witches

EDMUND ROBINSON, son of Ned of Roughs, set off from his Pendle Forest home on All Saints' Day to gather plums. He was caught up in one of the most fantastic witch stories of them all. The lad was about 11 years old, and it did not take him long to reach the orchard. As he gathered the fruit he saw two greyhounds running across the next field, moving towards him. One dog was black, and the other brown. They were similar in type and colour to animals belonging to local men.

Edmund stopped plum-gathering when the dogs made a fuss of him, and he patted their sleek heads. Each had a collar which shone like gold, and to each collar was attached a length of string. The Robinsons were not well off, and Edmund thought of the hares which abounded in the district. No-one was coming to claim the greyhounds immediately so he decided to take them coursing, and he led them to some open country. A hare rose from its "form" and lolloped away. Edmund shouted at the greyhounds, but they would not move, and the hare, accelerating quickly, was soon out of range. Annoyed by the lack of response, he tied the greyhounds to a small bush and began to beat them a switch. The black greyhound was mysteriously transformed into the wife of Dickenson, a neighbour of the Robinsons, and the brown greyhound turned itself into a small boy who was unknown to Edmund.

Young Robinson told his story on oath before Pendle magistrates in the February of 1633, 21 years after the big witch trial at Lancaster. His deposition was to send many more "witches" across the Bowland hills to Lancaster. When the greyhounds turned into humans, Edmund tried to run away, but Dickenson's wife beckoned him back. She produced a piece of silver, which she said he could have if he would keep the strange encounter a secret. Edmund refused, and said: "Nay, thou art a witch." The woman again reached into a pocket, and pulled out a bridle, which she placed on the head of the small boy. Now, instead of a boy, a white horse stood before Edmund and the woman. She lifted him on to the horse, clambered up behind him and they were carried to a house called Hoarstones, about a quarter of a mile away. As they approached, Edmund saw other people arriving on horses, which were tied up to a hedge near the house.

There were about 30 people at Hoarstones. A fire blazed in a hearth, and meat was being roasted. A young woman gave the lad some cooked meat and bread, together with a strange drink he sipped once but then left. The company made for a barn, and Edmund followed them. He saw six people kneeling, each pulling a rope. The ropes were fastened to the top of the barn. Edmund saw smoking flesh, butter in lumps and milk appearing from the ropes and falling into basins. When the first six people had finished, another six took over. The ugly faces being pulled by the people at the ropes scared the lad, and he stole away. A chase developed, but Edmund reached the highway at a fortunate time. Two horsemen were approaching, and scared off the pursuers. Edmund had recognised the wife of one Loynd and Jenet Davies: they and the wife of Dickenson had sometimes met in a croft close to his father's house, and they had scared him. One day Loynd's wife had been sitting part way up the chimney!

It was not the only shock that Edmund would have that day. His father told him to collect two cows which had to be tied up for the night. As he went for them he met a boy who quarrelled with him. There was a fight, during which Edmund noticed that the boy had a cloven foot. He had met Loynd's wife — she was standing on a bridge — and as he dashed away from her he met the boy again and was given a blow on his back, which made him cry. He had a spine-chilling encounter in the barn with three women who were removing pictures from a beam. What seemed to be thorns were sticking from the pictures. Edmund's father told the magistrates that when his son did not return promptly from attending to the cattle, he had gone in search of him, and had heard him crying. It was a quarter of an hour before the sobbing ended.

Edmund was now one of the best-known boys in the district. His fame did not end with his account of the witches he had met. He must have special gifts for finding witches, and so he was taken from church to church, and whoever was accused of witchcraft by him was promptly sent off for trial. In his travels, he crossed the border into Yorkshire. Webster, author of *Display of Witchcraft,* was curate at Kildwick church — the "Lang Kirk o' Craven" — when Edmund was brought to an afternoon service for the purpose of detecting any witches in the congregation. Webster noted that he was "set upon a stool to look about him, which moved some little disturbance in the congregation for a while. After prayers, I enquired what the matter was: the people told me that it was the boy that discovered witches; upon which I went to the house where he was to stay the night, and there I found him and two very unlikely persons, that did conduct him and manage the business.

"I desired to have some discourse with the boy in private but they utterly refused. Then in the presence of a great many people, I took the boy near me and said: 'Good boy, tell me truly and in earnest, didst thou see and hear such strange things at the meeting of witches as is reported by many thou didst relate?' But the two men, not giving the boy leave to answer, did pluck him from me, and said he had been examined by two such Justices of the Peace, and they did never ask him such a question. To whom I replied, the persons accused had therefore the more wrong."

Edmund's integrity survived. Seventeen witches had been arrested following the weird happenings with witch ropes in the barn at Hoarstones. Jenet Davies was charged with killing the wife of William Nutter. A Mary Spencer was arrested because she "caused a pail or cellocke to come to her, full of water, fourteen yards up a gill from a well." Margaret Johnson was accused of killing Henry Neape, and of washing and impairing the body of Jenet Shackleton. The only real proof against her were witch-marks. When these had been located, Margaret confessed. Seven or eight years before the Devil had appeared to her and she had exchanged her soul for his ready help. Margaret had been at the great gathering of witches which Edmund had observed at Hoarstones; there had been another gathering on the following Sunday.

A day had to come when the indiscriminate hanging of people suspected of witchcraft must end. Juries were still very prone to judge the accused guilty even before the evidence had been offered, or for the slenderest reasons. When Margaret Johnson and the others were up for trial, a verdict of guilty was quickly returned. The judge was not wholly satisfied. He managed to get a reprieve and some of the accused were sent to London for special consideration. The King, Charles I, was not as obsessed with witchcraft as his late father, James, had been, and when he was approached he ordered that a bishop should make a full investigation of the case and report on it.

Edmund was now on his own, separated from his father. He did not stand up to an examination for long before he confessed that his stories had been false. On All Saints' Day he was stealing plums, and his father had tried to cover up his crime by persuading him to lie. The career of witch-finder had been profitable for the Robinsons and from the Pendle district of his birth, Edmund had been taken far and wide to observe and condemn.

There is one important aspect of the story about which nothing is written — the fate of Edmund Robinson. Dr. Webster wrote: "By such wicked means and un-Christian practices, divers innocent persons lost their lives; and these wicked rogues wanted not greater persons (even of the ministry, too) that did authorise and encourage them in the diabolical courses; and the like in my time happened here in Lancashire; where divers, both men and women, were accused of supposed witchcraft, and were so un-Christian and unhumanly handled, as to be stripped stark naked and laid upon tables and beds to be searched for their supposed witch-marks; so barbarous and cruel acts both diabolical instigation, working upon ignorance and superstition, produce."

Witch Country Literature

WHEN THE WITCH TRIAL of 1612 was over, the Clerk of the Judges, Thomas Potts, gathered together the official notes, had a chat with a firm of printers, and dutifully — but with enormous bias against witches — published his account of *The Wonderful Discoverie of Witches in the Covntie of Lancaster*. The Judges wanted the story to become widely known. Potts obliged, using the evidence gathered earlier by the magistrates as well as that of the many witnesses who stood up and testified in the Assize Court. Both Potts and the printers worked with remarkable speed. Three months after the Pendle witches had been hanged, those with the will and the money were able to "read all about it".

After the initial horror of witchly doings about Pendle, something of a comic note appeared in Pendle's literature, with comedy on the subject being performed as early as 1634. A quotation attributed to a Lancashire Justice appeared in Thomas Shadwell's comedy of 1682. "No witches!" exclaimed a Justice. "Why, I myself have hanged above four-score." In more solemn vein was Dr. Webster's *Display of Witchcraft* (the full title was fantastically long), which included his encounter with young Robinson when he had been the curate at Kildwick, and affirmed "that there are many sorts of Deceivers and Imposters. And Divers persons under a passive Delusion of Melancholy and Fancy. But that there is a Corporal League made betwixt the Devil and the Witch . . . is utterly denied and disproved."

By the 19th century, the Pendle witches were given their full share of romance. Edwin Waugh, who wrote extensively about Lancashire life and humour, made one of his characters say "Thou'rt as fause as one o' th' Pendle Witches". William Harrison Ainsworth produced his massive romantic novel *The Lancashire Witches* (1848), the best-known book on the period ever since. Ainsworth dedicated his book to James Crossley, who was the President of the Cheetham Society and who in 1845 edited Pott's 1612 script, which is still the only first-hand account we have of the circumstances of that time. Ainsworth presented a great sweep of local history, with all the elements the Victorians loved best, from the fate of the last Abbot of Whalley to Jenet, "the last of the Lancashire Witches". The book was described as a romance.

There have been legions of poets, and one of them developed many of Pendle's eerie legends in verse, his tale of Malkin Tower introducing a Wizard Hildebrand, "skilled in every magic lore", and a young woman who was kept captive. Poets were inclined to take their readers far into the world of fancy. Some poets bordered on the ridiculous!

Mist over Pendle, which Robert Neill produced in 1951, is a stirring tale carrying greater conviction than Ainsworth's saga. A native of Manchester who has strong family connections with Colne, Mr. Neill served in the Navy during the last war. When he was stationed at a lonely base on the west coast of Scotland with some time on his hands, he began to read about the Pendle witches, trying to work out in his mind what really happened. Then, in 1950, when he was a teacher, he began to write about the witches with the object of clearing his head of this fascinating subject. He found that he had a novel on his hands. That novel, written in a year, was accepted by the second firm of publishers to whom it was sent. It also became the choice of an American book club.

Mr. Neill met a bookseller in one of the Lancashire cotton towns near Pendle. The bookseller had received an advance copy of *Mist over Pendle* from Hutchinsons, and he had read and liked it. Before he placed an order for the book he got out his bicycle and went round the various routes taken by the characters — just to make sure that they could be covered in accordance with the story. "Would it have mattered much if the routes had been wrong?" asked Mr. Neill. The bookseller replied: "Aye, it would here. They'd have brought book back!"

Last thoughts about Witches

IF YOU LIKE your pictures of witches romantic, then read no further. Despite the tales and legends of witches around and over Pendle (there has been such a welter of tales it is not easy to arrive at the true details), it is unlikely that witchcraft of the classic tradition was practised here. The witch stories which circulated, and the two families and their neighbours who latched on to them, did strike fear into the hearts of the Pendle Foresters three hundred and seventy years ago, but witchcraft may have been just a cover for petty crime. You can think of the Demdikes and the Chattoxes as people tuned into the Devil, or as two family gangs of miscreants who, when they eventually quarrelled after years of co-existence, contributed to each other's downfall by rash of accusation about evil doings.

A most helpful booklet for those who would like to strip away much of the fiction and expose the few available facts was written by Mr. Walter Bennett, and published by the county borough of Burnley in 1957. He wrote: "In an age of superstition, when belief in witchcraft was widespread, a suspicion became a rumour and then an indisputable fact so that it was almost inevitable that such characters as Demdike and Chattox, cunning, cruel and living in dire poverty, should be regarded as witches. Possibly the two old women traded on their evil reputations to extort a living more easily from their frightened neighbours; possibly, too, they made images and recited charms to enhance their notoriety . . ."

One peculiarity about the witches was the way they tended to operate in covens (with thirteen as the traditional number), and persisted in certain limited geographical locations. Pendle was one of them. There may have been witch talk in this area before the Demdike–Chattox clique became prominent; there was certainly talk for long, long years afterwards, as though some germ had settled here, to lie dormant for a while and then become virulent again. The Pendle Foresters had a real fear of witches and clung to their charms until quite recent times.

Their caution was understandable. The time when the witches flourished around Pendle and elsewhere was a time when the yeoman farmer was coming into his own. The dissolution of the monasteries years before had brought about a great liberalisation of ideas and of trade; now the common man had his chance to be his own master, and through the efforts of his hands to flourish in wealth and status. Some were to reflect their new power and pride in the building of stone homes and outbuildings which dated mainly from the latter part of the 17th century and through into the 18th.

During the reigns of Elizabeth and James I, the capital value of stock was increasing. To lose a cow or even a sheep was a tragedy for the smaller men, and those who were farming in a big way were sensitive to the health of their stock, which were being housed together in greater numbers. Farming with stock had its hazards, as it has today. There were unaccountable variations in the yield of milk, cows aborted their calves, and on some days milk refused to be converted into good butter or cheese. In a world which was yet to have a veterinary science, it was easy and convenient to blame witches or other evil spirits for ill luck. It was the witch who, roaming the countryside in the guise of a hare, kept down milk production by drawing off milk from the teats of cattle being pastured out-of-doors. The witch entered the outbuildings, spreading disease among the stock. The witch, by casting spells, could affect cream in a churn so that it refused to turn.

If the Pendle witches were not in the classical mould they seemed to have a real hankering after the "black art"; once infected with an interest in the supernatural, they would pass on that infection to others close at hand, so that the ideas were perpetuated.

Was the Pendle witch that wise person who had a part to play in a simple society where medicine was rudimentary and veterinary science not yet properly defined? James Crossley (1835) wrote: "He who visits Pendle may yet find that charms are generally resorted to amongst the lower classes . . . that each small hamlet has a peculiar and gifted personage . . . that the wiseman and wisewoman, the white witches of our ancestors, still continue their investigations of truth undisturbed by the rural police or the progress of the schoolmaster." It's just that some people were not content with wisdom, and turned to extortion.

Nineteen Names

THE 19 WITCHES who were tried at Lancaster in August, 1612.

From Pendle. Old Chattox (Anne Whittle), Elizabeth Davies, James Davies, Anne Redfern (acquitted), Alice Nutter, Katherine Hewitt, John Bulcock and Jane Bulcock, (the Bulcocks were acquitted), Alizon Davies.

From Padiham. Margaret Pearson.

From Windle, St. Helens. Isobel Roby.

From the Salmesbury Area. Jennet Bierley, Ellen Bierley, Jane Southworth, John Ramsden, Elizabeth Astley, Alice Gray, Isabel Sidegraves, Lawrence Haye. (A "not guilty" verdict was returned in the case of those from Salmesbury).